PRINCIPLES FOR DEALING WITH THE ECONOMY AND BUDGETING

A Guide to Managing Your Finances During an Economic Recession and Navigating Prosperity

GLENN S. SHERMAN &

LINDA M. BARNETTE

Table of contents

Introduction:

In times of economic uncertainty and recession, budgeting becomes more crucial than ever. A recession can bring about financial challenges, making it imperative for individuals and families to manage their finances wisely. This comprehensive guide will explore the art of budgeting during a recession, offering practical tips and insights to help you weather the storm and emerge financially stable.

This book is your go-to resource for practical tips, real-life case studies, and step-by-step guidance on financial planning, investment, and risk management. Whether you're an individual seeking to secure your family's financial stability or a business owner striving to safeguard your company's success, this book provides the knowledge and tools you need.

Chapter 1

Understanding Recession

1.1 Defining a Recession

A recession is an economic downturn characterized by a significant decline in economic activity. It typically involves a drop in gross domestic product (GDP), rising unemployment rates, reduced consumer spending, and a decrease in business investments. Recession can result from various factors, including financial crises, high inflation, supply shocks, or decreased consumer confidence.

Governments and central banks often respond to recessions by implementing fiscal and monetary policies to stimulate the economy. Fiscal policies involve measures like tax cuts and increased government spending, while monetary policies can include lowering interest rates or implementing quantitative easing to encourage borrowing and investment.

Recessions can have far-reaching social and economic impacts, including increased poverty, reduced job opportunities, and financial hardship for many individuals and businesses. They can also impact global markets and trade.

It's important to note that the severity and duration of a recession can vary, and economic indicators are closely monitored to identify and respond to these downturns effectively. Economists and policymakers continually study and analyze recession patterns to develop strategies for mitigating their effects and promoting economic stability.

1.2 Economic Indicators and signs

Economic indicators are essential tools for governments, businesses, and investors to gauge the health and direction of an economy. They provide valuable insights into various aspects of economic performance, from overall growth to the stability of financial markets.

However, these indicators are not just for informational purposes; they also serve as critical warning signs that can signal potential economic trouble on the horizon. In this article, we will explore the significance of economic indicators and how they can act as early warning signs for economic instability.

Understanding Economic Indicators

Economic indicators are statistics or data points that provide information about different aspects of an economy. They can be broadly categorized into leading, lagging, and coincident indicators. Each of these serves a unique role in offering insights into the economic landscape.

1. Leading Indicators: These indicators tend to change before the economy as a whole changes. They are used to predict future economic trends. Examples include new housing permits, stock market performance, and consumer confidence. A downturn in these indicators may signal an impending

economic slowdown.

2. Lagging Indicators: These indicators change after the economy as a whole, making them useful for confirming long-term trends. Examples include unemployment rates and corporate profits. When these indicators start to decline, it might indicate that the economy is already in a downturn.

3. Coincident Indicators: Coincident indicators change at the same time as the overall economy. They are used to confirm the current state of

the economy. Examples include industrial production and retail sales.

Warning Signs in Economic Indicators

Economic indicators can serve as early warning signs for a variety of economic issues, including recessions, inflation, and financial crises. Here are some key warning signs to watch for:

1. Rising Unemployment: A sudden increase in unemployment rates can

be a clear indication of an economic downturn. This can lead to reduced consumer spending and lower overall economic activity.

2. Inverted Yield Curve: When short-term interest rates rise above long-term rates, it can signal an impending recession. This phenomenon, known as an inverted yield curve, has historically been a reliable predictor of economic trouble.

3. Declining Consumer Confidence: A drop in consumer confidence can

indicate that people are less optimistic about the economy's future, leading to reduced spending and investment.

4. Stock Market Volatility: Sharp declines in stock markets can signal investor uncertainty and potentially foreshadow economic instability.

5. Increasing Debt Levels: Rising government, corporate, or household debt levels can be a warning sign of future financial crises or economic instability.

6. Declining Manufacturing and Industrial Production: A slump in manufacturing and industrial output may indicate reduced demand and a weakening economy.

7. Inflation Surge: Rapidly increasing inflation can erode purchasing power and create uncertainty in financial markets, potentially leading to economic problems.

8. Balance of Trade Deficits: Persistent trade deficits can be a warning sign, indicating that a country is importing more than it's

exporting, which can strain its economy.

1.3 Impact on Personal Finances

The impact of a recession on personal finances can be profound and far-reaching. Recession, typically defined as a significant decline in economic activity that lasts for an extended period, often results in a domino effect of financial challenges for individuals and families. In this article, we will explore the various ways in which a recession can affect personal finances and offer some strategies to navigate these difficult times.

1. Job Loss and Income Reduction:

One of the most immediate and severe consequences of a recession is a rise in unemployment. Many businesses struggle to survive during economic downturns and may resort to layoffs or hiring freezes. Individuals who lose their jobs or experience reduced hours face a substantial decrease in income, making it challenging to meet their financial obligations.

2. Investment Decline:

A recession can have a detrimental effect on investment portfolios. Stock markets tend to take a hit during economic downturns, causing a decline in the value of stocks and other investments. This can result in substantial financial losses for those heavily invested in the market.

3. Housing Market Fluctuations:

The real estate market is closely tied to the overall economy. During a recession, housing prices may fall, making it difficult for homeowners to sell their properties or even leading to negative equity. For those looking to buy a home, this might be an opportune time, but it can be a risky venture if job stability is uncertain.

4. Increased Cost of Borrowing:

The central banks often respond to recessions by lowering interest rates to stimulate economic activity. However, banks may tighten lending standards, making it challenging for individuals to access credit. Those who can obtain loans may face higher interest rates, increasing the cost of borrowing.

5. Reduced Consumer Spending:

During a recession, people tend to cut back on discretionary spending. This can lead to decreased demand for products and services, which can, in turn, impact businesses and potentially result in more job losses.

6. Impact on Retirement Savings:

Individuals saving for retirement

can see their plans disrupted. As mentioned earlier, investment portfolios may suffer losses, affecting long-term retirement savings. Some may be forced to delay their retirement plans.

7. Healthcare and Insurance Costs:

Healthcare expenses and insurance premiums can rise during a recession. For many, this additional financial burden can strain already tight budgets.

8. Emotional and Mental Health

Effects:

The stress and uncertainty associated with a recession can take a toll on individuals' emotional and mental well-being. This, in turn, can impact their ability to make sound financial decisions and maintain a clear financial strategy.

So, what can individuals do to mitigate the impact of a recession on their personal finances?

1. Emergency Fund:

Having an emergency fund is

crucial. It can provide a financial cushion in case of job loss or unexpected expenses.

2. Budgeting:

Creating a budget and managing expenses diligently can help individuals weather financial challenges during a recession.

3. Debt Management:

Reducing and managing debt can provide financial relief. Consider consolidating high-interest debts and exploring options for loan deferment or forbearance.

4. Diversify Investments:

Diversifying your investment portfolio can help spread risk and reduce the impact of market downturns.

5. Explore Additional Income Sources:

Freelancing, part-time work, or side gigs can provide an additional source of income during tough times.

6. Evaluate Housing Decisions:

Consider your housing situation and whether it aligns with your current financial circumstances. Renting or downsizing might be more prudent during a recession.

7. Healthcare and Insurance Review:

Review your healthcare and insurance plans to ensure you have adequate coverage without unnecessary costs.

8. Seek Professional Advice:

Consult with a financial advisor or counselor who can help you develop a personalized financial strategy.

The impact of a recession on personal finances can be substantial and multifaceted. However, with careful planning, budgeting, and proactive measures, individuals can navigate these challenging times and emerge with their financial well-being intact. Staying informed about economic trends and seeking professional advice when needed are essential components of effective financial management during a recession.

Chapter 2

The Importance of Budgeting

2.1 The Role of Budgeting

Budgeting plays a crucial role during a recession. As economic downturns bring financial uncertainty and challenges, effective budgeting becomes a strategic tool for individuals, businesses, and governments to navigate through turbulent times. In this article, we will explore the multifaceted role of budgeting in managing finances during a recession.

1. Financial Stability: The primary role of budgeting during a recession is to maintain financial stability. It helps individuals and families to assess their income, expenses, and savings. By creating a well-structured budget, they can ensure that they do not spend more than they earn, thus preventing a financial crisis.

2. Cost Control: In the business world, budgeting is vital for cost

control. Companies need to carefully allocate resources, reduce unnecessary expenditures, and streamline their operations. A well-managed budget can enable businesses to cut costs without compromising on essential activities, helping them weather the economic storm.

3. Resource Allocation: Governments, too, rely on budgeting to allocate resources efficiently during a recession. This includes funding essential public services, such as

healthcare and unemployment benefits. A budget ensures that resources are distributed in a way that maximizes their impact on economic recovery.

4. Planning and Prioritization: In times of recession, individuals, businesses, and governments need to plan and prioritize their financial commitments. A budget helps in identifying critical expenses, such as mortgage payments, payroll, and debt servicing, while postponing or reducing non-essential spending.

5. Debt Management: Recessions often lead to increased levels of debt for many individuals and organizations. A budget can serve as a tool for managing existing debts and avoiding the accumulation of additional debt. By making calculated decisions on how to allocate funds, it's possible to gradually pay off debts and avoid financial distress.

6. Cash Flow Management: Managing cash flow is critical during a recession. Businesses need to

ensure they have enough cash on hand to meet immediate obligations, while individuals must cover their daily expenses. Budgeting helps in monitoring and forecasting cash flow, allowing for better financial decisions.

7. Emergency Funds: A well-planned budget during normal times should include provisions for emergency funds. These reserves can be invaluable during a recession, providing a financial safety net for unexpected circumstances, such as

job loss or unexpected business expenses.

8. Investment Decisions: For individuals with investments, budgeting can help in making informed decisions about their portfolios. In a recession, it may be necessary to rebalance or diversify investments to reduce risk and protect capital.

9. **Adaptability**: A recession may necessitate swift changes in financial strategies. Budgets should be flexible and adaptable to

accommodate evolving circumstances. This can mean adjusting spending priorities or reallocating resources to respond effectively to changing economic conditions.

10. Communication and Transparency: In a corporate context, budgeting fosters transparency and clear communication. It allows leaders to communicate with employees, shareholders, and stakeholders about financial plans and the steps

being taken to ensure the organization's survival and recovery.

11. Long-Term Sustainability: Beyond immediate crisis management, budgeting also plays a role in long-term financial sustainability. It encourages forward -thinking and the development of strategies to ensure economic resilience against future recessions.

Budgeting is a fundamental tool for individuals, businesses, and governments when facing a recession. It provides a structured framework for financial decision-making, helps in stabilizing finances, and allows for adaptability in turbulent times. By recognizing the importance of budgeting during a recession and implementing effective budgeting practices, individuals and organizations can mitigate the impact of economic downturns and work towards a more secure financial future.

2.2 Financial Goals and Priorities

Financial goals and priorities are integral aspects of our lives. They shape our financial decisions, influence our savings and spending patterns, and ultimately determine our financial well-being. Setting clear financial goals and establishing priorities is a critical step toward achieving financial success and security. In this comprehensive exploration, we'll delve into the significance of financial goals and priorities, how to set them, and strategies to achieve them.

Understanding Financial Goals:

Financial goals are specific, measurable, and time-bound objectives that individuals or households set to attain a desired financial outcome. These goals vary widely from person to person, as they are deeply rooted in personal aspirations and circumstances. Some common financial goals include:

1. Emergency Fund: Building an emergency fund is often the first financial goal people set. It provides a financial safety net for unexpected

expenses, such as medical bills or car repairs.

2. Debt Repayment: Paying off high-interest debts, like credit card balances or student loans, is a crucial financial goal. Reducing debt can free up funds for other priorities.

3. Retirement Savings: Planning for retirement is a long-term financial goal. Saving for retirement early allows for compound interest to work in your favor.

4. Homeownership: Purchasing a

home is a significant financial goal for many. It often requires a substantial down payment and ongoing mortgage payments.

5. Education: Saving for education, whether for yourself, your children, or grandchildren, is another important goal. It can help reduce the burden of student loans.

6. Investing: Growing your wealth through investments is a common financial goal. It can include saving for a major purchase or building wealth for the future.

7. Travel and Leisure: Setting aside funds for vacations and leisure activities can provide a better work-life balance.

Establishing Financial Priorities:

Once you've identified your financial goals, it's essential to establish priorities. Not all goals can be addressed simultaneously, and prioritization ensures that you allocate your resources effectively. Here are some considerations when setting priorities:

1. Urgency: Goals that are more time-sensitive, like emergency savings or debt repayment, should often take precedence.

2. Interest Rates: High-interest debts should be a top priority, as they can quickly erode your financial health.

3. Longevity: Long-term goals, such as retirement or education savings, require consistent contributions over time, so they should be a priority.

4. Life Events: Major life events like

marriage, childbirth, or buying a home can significantly impact your financial priorities.

5. Risk Tolerance: Your risk tolerance and investment horizon should guide your investment priorities.

Strategies to Achieve Financial Goals:

Once you've set your financial goals and established priorities, it's crucial to implement strategies to achieve them. Here are some effective strategies:

1. Budgeting: Creating and sticking

to a budget helps you manage your income and expenses. It ensures that you allocate funds to meet your financial goals.

2. Automated Savings: Setting up automatic transfers to savings or investment accounts ensures that you consistently save for your goals.

3. Debt Repayment Plans: Develop a structured plan to pay off debts. The snowball or avalanche method can be effective, depending on your circumstances.

4. Investing Wisely: Diversify your investment portfolio and consider your risk tolerance and time horizon when making investment decisions.

5. Continuous Learning: Stay informed about personal finance and investment strategies to make informed decisions.

6. Regular Review: Periodically review and adjust your financial goals and priorities as your circumstances change.

7. Seek Professional Advice: Consult

with financial advisors or planners for guidance on complex financial goals, such as retirement or estate planning.

Financial goals and priorities play a fundamental role in shaping our financial well-being and future. By setting clear goals, establishing priorities, and implementing effective strategies, you can work toward achieving financial success and security. Remember that your financial goals are unique to your situation, and it's essential to adapt them as life evolves.

2.3 Emergency Funds

Emergency Funds: Your Financial Lifesaver

In the world of personal finance, few concepts are as universally important as the emergency fund. An emergency fund is a financial safety net, a stash of money set aside specifically for unexpected expenses or life's curveballs. Whether it's a medical emergency, a sudden job loss, a car breakdown, or a home repair, having an emergency fund can be your lifeline during times of financial distress.

What Is an Emergency Fund?

An emergency fund is a readily accessible savings account that provides you with a financial cushion when unforeseen expenses arise. It's designed to cover urgent, non-negotiable costs that you didn't anticipate, helping you avoid going into debt, relying on credit cards, or liquidating investments at inopportune times.

The Importance of an Emergency Fund

1. Financial Peace of Mind: One of the primary benefits of having an emergency fund is the peace of mind it offers. Knowing that you have a financial buffer to weather unexpected storms can significantly reduce stress and anxiety in your life.

2. Protection from Debt: Without an emergency fund, many people resort to borrowing money to cover

unexpected expenses. This can lead to high-interest debt, which can be financially crippling. An emergency fund acts as a shield against debt and helps you maintain your financial independence.

3. Maintaining Financial Goals: Your long-term financial goals, such as retirement savings or buying a home, can be severely derailed if you're constantly dipping into your regular savings to cover emergencies. An emergency fund allows you to protect these goals and stay on

track.

4. Avoiding Hasty Decisions: Financial emergencies can create a sense of urgency that may lead to hasty, ill-advised decisions. With an emergency fund, you can take the time to make more considered choices and avoid costly mistakes.

Building an Emergency Fund

Building an emergency fund takes time and discipline, but it's an essential part of financial planning. Here's how to get started:

1. Set a Goal: Determine how much you want to have in your emergency fund. A common guideline is to aim for three to six months' worth of living expenses, but your specific circumstances may warrant more or less.

2. Create a Budget: Track your income and expenses to find room for saving. Make sure to allocate a portion of your income to your emergency fund regularly.

3. Open a Separate Account: It's a good idea to keep your emergency

fund separate from your regular savings or checking accounts. This separation can help prevent you from spending the money impulsively.

4. Automate Savings: Set up automatic transfers from your primary account to your emergency fund. This ensures that you consistently contribute to it.

5. Use Windfalls: Whenever you receive unexpected money, like a bonus, tax refund, or gift, consider allocating a portion of it to your

emergency fund.

6. Cut Unnecessary Expenses: Review your spending habits and cut back on non-essential expenses to boost your emergency fund more quickly.

Using Your Emergency Fund

An emergency fund should only be used for genuine emergencies. Here are some guidelines for when to dip into your fund:

1. Medical Expenses: If you have an unexpected medical bill that you

can't cover with your regular income, it's a valid use of your emergency fund.

2. Job Loss: If you lose your job or face a significant reduction in income, your emergency fund can help cover essential living expenses until you get back on your feet.

3. Car Repairs: Necessary car repairs can be costly, and having a working vehicle may be essential for your daily life.

4. Home Repairs: Issues like a

leaking roof or a broken furnace can't wait and should be covered by your emergency fund.

5. Legal Emergencies: Unexpected legal issues may require financial resources, making your emergency fund invaluable.

6. Natural Disasters: In the unfortunate event of a natural disaster, your emergency fund can help you recover and rebuild.

Replenishing Your Emergency Fund

Once you've used your emergency

fund, it's crucial to replenish it as soon as possible. The sooner you rebuild your safety net, the better protected you are against future unexpected expenses.

An emergency fund is not a luxury; it's a necessity for every individual or household. It's a financial tool that can provide stability and security during life's most challenging moments. Building and maintaining an emergency fund is a responsible and prudent choice that can make a world of difference in your financial well-being. Remember, it's not a matter of if an emergency will happen, but when. So, start building your emergency fund today to safeguard your financial future.

Chapter 3

Creating a Recession-Proof Budget

3.1 Assessing Current Financial Situation

A critical aspect of maintaining financial stability and planning for the future is regularly assessing your current financial situation. This process involves a comprehensive evaluation of your income, expenses, assets, and liabilities, enabling you to make informed decisions about your financial well-being. Whether you're an individual, a family, or a business, understanding your financial health is essential for setting and achieving your financial goals.

1. Income Analysis:

Begin by examining your sources of income. This includes your salary, wages, investments, rental income, or any other monetary inflows. Calculate your total monthly and yearly income, ensuring you account for all revenue streams.

2. Expense Tracking:

Document and categorize your expenses. This includes fixed costs like mortgage or rent, utilities, insurance, groceries, and discretionary spending on entertainment, dining out, and more. Identifying areas where you can reduce expenses can be beneficial.

3. Budgeting:

Create a budget based on your income and expenses. This provides a roadmap for managing your finances and ensures that you live within your means. Adjust your budget as needed to align with your financial goals.

4. Savings and Investments:

Review your savings and investment accounts. Determine if you're saving enough for your short-term and long-term goals, such as emergencies, retirement, or major purchases.

5. Debt Assessment:

Evaluate your outstanding debts, including credit cards, loans, and mortgages. Determine the interest rates and monthly payments. Develop a strategy to pay off high-interest debt and manage your overall debt load.

6. Assets and Liabilities:

List your assets, including real estate, vehicles, investments, and valuable possessions. Similarly, document your liabilities, such as outstanding loans and mortgages. Calculate your net worth by subtracting liabilities from assets.

7. Emergency Fund:

Ensure you have an adequate emergency fund in place to cover unexpected expenses. Financial advisors typically recommend having three to six months' worth of living expenses saved.

8. Financial Goals:

Define your short-term and long-term financial objectives. These can range from buying a home, funding education, saving for retirement, or starting a business. Setting specific, measurable, achievable, relevant, and time-bound (SMART) goals is essential.

9. Regular Monitoring:

Continuously monitor your financial situation. Regularly update your budget, track your progress toward goals, and make adjustments as necessary. Life circumstances can change, and your financial plan should adapt accordingly.

Assessing your current financial situation is a fundamental step toward achieving financial stability and realizing your financial goals. It empowers you to make informed decisions, manage your resources efficiently, and build a secure financial future. Regularly reviewing and adjusting your financial status ensures that you remain on the path to financial success.

3.2   Reducing   Non-Essential Expenses

In   an   era   of   ever-increasing

consumerism, it's easy to fall into the trap of spending on non-essential items and experiences. These expenses can add up quickly, impacting your financial health and potentially leading to debt and financial stress. To regain control over your finances, it's crucial to identify and reduce non-essential expenses. In this guide, we'll explore practical steps and strategies to help you cut back on discretionary spending and prioritize financial well-being.

1. Create a Detailed Budget:

Start by creating a comprehensive budget that outlines your monthly income and expenses. Categorize your expenses into two groups: essential and non-essential. Essential expenses include items like housing, groceries, utilities, and transportation. Non-essential expenses are those that you can cut back on without significantly affecting your quality of life, such as dining out, entertainment, and impulse purchases.

2. Prioritize Your Financial Goals:

Setting clear financial goals is essential for reducing non-essential expenses. Whether you're saving for a vacation, paying off debt, or building an emergency fund, having specific objectives can motivate you to cut back on discretionary spending.

3. Identify Non-Essential Expenses:

Review your spending habits to pinpoint areas where you can cut back. Common non-essential expenses include eating out frequently, subscription services, impulse purchases, and expensive hobbies. Use bank and credit card statements to track your spending and identify trends.

4. Develop a Spending Plan:

Once you've identified non-essential expenses, create a spending plan that allocates a specific amount of your income to each category. Be realistic and allocate more funds to essential expenses while limiting non-essential categories.

5. Automate Savings:

Make saving a non-negotiable part of your budget by setting up automated transfers to a savings account. This way, you're less likely to spend the money on non-essential items.

6. Cut Back Gradually:

It's important to be realistic about reducing non-essential expenses. Abruptly cutting out all discretionary spending can be challenging and discouraging. Start by gradually reducing these expenses, and over time, you'll adjust to a more frugal lifestyle.

7. Review Subscriptions:

Assess your monthly subscription services, from streaming platforms to gym memberships. Cancel any that you're not using regularly or consider sharing subscriptions with family or friends to split costs.

8. Shop Mindfully:

When shopping for non-essential items, adopt a more mindful

approach. Ask yourself if the purchase is a want or a need, and whether it aligns with your financial goals. Delaying purchases and making shopping lists can help curb impulse buying.

9. Cook at Home:

Dining out or ordering takeout can quickly drain your budget. Cooking at home not only saves money but also allows you to eat healthier and control portion sizes.

10. Seek Affordable Alternatives:

Explore cost-effective alternatives to expensive activities or hobbies. For instance, if you love working out, consider home workouts or outdoor activities instead of an expensive gym membership.

11. Use Cash Envelopes:

Some people find it helpful to use the cash envelope system. Allocate a specific amount of cash for non-essential expenses each week or month, and once it's gone, you can't spend more until the next budgeting period.

12. Find Free or Low-Cost Entertainment:

Look for free or low-cost entertainment options in your community. Many cities offer free concerts, events, and parks for enjoyment without spending much.

13. Compare Prices and Shop Smart:

Before making any non-essential purchase, compare prices, look for discounts, and consider buying generic brands or used items. There are plenty of online tools and apps that can help you find the best deals.

14. Review and Adjust Regularly:

Your financial situation and priorities may change over time. Regularly review your budget and adjust it to reflect your current goals and circumstances.

15. Build an Emergency Fund:

A crucial part of financial health is having an emergency fund. Set aside a portion of your savings to create a financial safety net for unexpected expenses, reducing the need to dip into non-essential spending.

16. Seek Support and Accountability:

Discuss your financial goals with a trusted friend or family member who can provide support and hold you accountable for your spending decisions.

Reducing non-essential expenses is a key step toward financial security and achieving your financial goals. By creating a budget, prioritizing your financial objectives, and making mindful spending decisions, you can take control of your finances, reduce financial stress, and work towards a more secure and prosperous future. Remember, it's not about sacrificing all the things you love but rather making more intentional choices about how you allocate your resources.

3.3 Prioritizing Necessities

A Key to a Balanced Life

In our fast-paced, modern world, it's easy to become overwhelmed by the demands and distractions of daily life. Whether it's work, social obligations, or personal pursuits, it can be challenging to strike a balance. One essential skill for maintaining that balance is prioritizing necessities. By identifying and focusing on what truly matters, we can lead more fulfilling, purpose-driven lives.

1. Defining Necessities

Before we delve into the art of prioritization, it's crucial to understand what we mean by "necessities." Necessities are the fundamental elements of life that we cannot do without. These may vary from person to person but often include:

a. Basic Needs: Food, water, shelter, and clothing are fundamental to survival. Ensuring access to these necessities is our first responsibility.

b. Health and Well-Being: Physical and mental health should be a top priority. Regular exercise, a balanced diet, and adequate sleep are critical components.

c. Relationships: Human connections are essential for our emotional well-being. Nurturing relationships with family, friends, and loved ones is a necessity.

d. Career and Financial Stability: Work and income are necessary for sustaining our way of life. This includes managing finances, saving, and planning for the future.

e. Personal Growth and Fulfillment: Pursuing interests, passions, and self-improvement is integral to leading a fulfilling life.

2. The Process of Prioritization

To prioritize necessities effectively, you need a systematic approach. Here are some steps to help you get started:

a. Identify Your Necessities: Make a list of what you consider to be your necessities. This can help clarify your values and goals.

b. Rank Your Necessities: Prioritize these necessities by order of importance. Consider which ones are vital for your well-being and happiness.

c. Eliminate Unnecessary Distractions: Identify activities, commitments, or possessions that aren't aligned with your priorities. These can be distractions that hinder you from focusing on what truly matters.

d. Time Management: Allocate your time according to your priorities. Create a schedule that ensures you dedicate sufficient time to essential areas of your life.

e. Set Goals: Establish clear, actionable goals related to your priorities. This can help you stay on track and measure your progress.

3. Benefits of Prioritizing Necessities

Prioritizing necessities offers numerous benefits:

a. Reduced Stress: Focusing on what truly matters reduces the stress of juggling too many obligations.

b. Improved Well-Being: Addressing your basic needs and nurturing relationships can enhance your overall quality of life.

c. Increased Productivity: Concentrating on priorities enables you to work more efficiently, making the most of your time and energy.

d. Greater Fulfillment: By aligning your actions with your values, you'll experience a sense of purpose and fulfillment.

e. Better Decision-Making: Prioritization helps you make more informed decisions, as you are clear about your goals and what matters most to you.

4. Challenges and Pitfalls

While prioritizing necessities is essential, it's not always easy. Some common challenges and pitfalls include:

a. Overcommitment: The temptation to take on too many commitments can divert your focus from what truly matters.

b. External Influences: Societal pressures, peer expectations, and the lure of material possessions can lead you astray.

c. Neglecting Self-Care: In the pursuit of external goals, it's easy to overlook self-care, which is fundamental to our well-being.

d. Resistance to Change: Shifting your priorities may require changing long-established habits, which can be challenging.

In a world teeming with distractions and demands, prioritizing necessities is the compass that can guide us toward a balanced, meaningful life. It's a process that allows us to focus on what truly matters, improve our overall well-being, and pursue our goals with purpose and intention. By taking the time to identify, rank, and allocate resources to our necessities, we can lead more fulfilling lives that align with our values and aspirations. So, take a step back, evaluate your priorities, and begin the journey to a more balanced and purpose-driven life.

3.4 Allocating Funds for Savings and

Investments

Financial security and independence are crucial goals for many individuals and families. One of the key strategies to achieve these goals is allocating funds for savings and investments. Properly managing your money by setting aside a portion for both short-term savings and long-term investments is essential for building wealth and securing your financial future.

1. The Importance of Saving and Investing

Saving and investing are distinct but interrelated financial activities. Saving involves setting aside a portion of your income for future use, typically in relatively safe and easily accessible accounts, such as savings accounts or certificates of deposit. On the other hand, investing involves putting your money to work in various financial instruments with the goal of earning a higher return over the long term, even though it may involve a higher level of risk.

Savings provide a safety net for unexpected expenses and emergencies. Having a readily available fund can help you avoid taking on high-interest debt when the unexpected occurs. Investments, on the other hand, help your money grow over time, beating the effects of inflation and providing financial security in the long run.

2. Setting Clear Financial Goals

Before you can effectively allocate funds for savings and investments, it's essential to establish clear financial goals. These goals can be short-term or long-term. Short-term goals might include building an emergency fund, saving for a vacation, or a down payment on a house. Long-term goals could be retirement planning, saving for your child's education, or achieving financial independence.

Defining these goals will help you determine how much you need to save and invest and the time frame in which you plan to achieve them.

3. Creating a Budget

To allocate funds for savings and investments, you need to create and stick to a budget. A budget is a financial plan that outlines your income and expenses. By tracking your expenses and ensuring that your income exceeds your outflows, you can identify how much money is available for saving and investing. Creating a budget helps you gain control over your finances and make informed decisions about allocating funds.

4. The 50/30/20 Rule

One popular approach to allocating funds is the 50/30/20 rule. This rule suggests that you should allocate 50% of your income to needs (such as housing, utilities, and groceries), 30% to wants (like dining out and entertainment), and 20% to savings and investments. This guideline provides a structured way to ensure you are saving and investing a significant portion of your income while still allowing for discretionary spending.

5. Diversification in Investments

When it comes to investing, diversification is a crucial strategy. Diversifying your investments means spreading your money across different asset classes, such as stocks, bonds, real estate, and other investment vehicles. Diversification helps reduce risk because it minimizes the impact of poor performance in any single investment.

6. Types of Savings and Investment Accounts

Savings accounts and certificates

of deposit (CDs) are ideal for short-term savings. These accounts are low-risk and provide easy access to your funds. They are typically offered by banks and credit unions.

For long-term investments, you can consider options like:

- Stocks: Represent ownership in a company and can offer high returns but come with higher risk.

- Bonds: Are loans to entities like governments or corporations and are generally considered lower risk than stocks.

- Mutual Funds: Pool money from multiple investors to invest in a diversified portfolio of stocks, bonds, or other securities.

- Real Estate: Investing in physical properties, such as homes, commercial buildings, or real estate investment trusts (REITs).

7. Regular Monitoring and Adjustment

Your financial situation and goals

can change over time. Therefore, it's important to regularly monitor your savings and investment accounts, and adjust your allocations as needed. You may need to rebalance your portfolio to ensure that it aligns with your risk tolerance and financial goals.

8. Tax-Efficient Saving and Investing

Being tax-savvy is also an important aspect of allocating funds for savings and investments. Taking advantage of tax-advantaged accounts such as 401(k)s, IRAs, and

529 plans can help you reduce your tax liability while building wealth for retirement and education expenses.

9. The Power of Compound Interest

The sooner you start allocating funds for investments, the more you can benefit from the power of compound interest. Compound interest allows your investments to grow not just on your initial capital but also on the returns earned over time. This exponential growth is a powerful wealth-building tool.

Allocating funds for savings and investments is a fundamental step toward achieving financial security and independence. By setting clear goals, creating a budget, diversifying investments, and regularly monitoring your progress, you can make informed decisions that will help you secure your financial future and meet your financial aspirations. Remember that there is no one-size-fits-all approach, and it's important to tailor your savings and investment strategy to your individual needs and circumstances.

Chapter 4

Cutting Costs Wisely

4.1 Meal Planning and Grocery Shopping

Meal planning and grocery shopping are two integral components of maintaining a healthy, efficient, and cost-effective lifestyle. These practices not only save time and money but also play a crucial role in promoting good health and reducing food waste. In this comprehensive guide, we will explore the benefits of meal planning and offer practical tips for effective grocery shopping.

The Benefits of Meal Planning

1. Saves Time

Meal planning allows you to make the most of your time. By deciding what to eat in advance, you reduce the need for impromptu decisions when you're hungry, which often lead to unhealthy food choices or eating out. Planning meals can be as simple as making a weekly menu or as detailed as prepping ingredients in advance.

2. Saves Money

One of the most significant financial benefits of meal planning is that it helps you avoid unnecessary food expenses. When you plan your meals, you're less likely to buy items that you won't use, and you can take advantage of sales and discounts. You can also buy ingredients in bulk, which can be more cost-effective.

3. Reduces Food Waste

Meal planning can help reduce food waste, a significant environmental and economic concern. By carefully choosing recipes and portioning meals, you can ensure that you use up the ingredients you purchase, reducing the amount of food that ends up in the trash.

4. Promotes Healthier Eating

Meal planning puts you in control of your diet. It allows you to make healthier choices by incorporating a variety of nutritious foods and controlling portion sizes. When you plan meals, it's easier to avoid the temptation of fast food or unhealthy snacks.

Tips for Effective Meal Planning

1. Set Realistic Goals

Start with achievable goals. If you're new to meal planning, consider planning just a few meals a week and gradually work your way up. It's essential to create a plan that fits your lifestyle.

2. Create a Weekly Menu

Planning a week's worth of meals at a time is a common approach. Write down breakfast, lunch, dinner, and snacks for each day. This will help you ensure a balanced diet and make grocery lists more manageable.

3. Check Your Pantry

Before you head to the grocery store, review your pantry, fridge, and freezer. This helps you identify items you already have and need to use up, reducing waste and saving money.

4. Plan for Leftovers

Intentionally cooking extra food to have as leftovers for the next day's lunch or dinner is an excellent time-saving and money-saving strategy.

The Art of Grocery Shopping

1. Make a List

Create a detailed grocery list based on your meal plan. Organize the list by categories such as produce, dairy, meat, and pantry staples. Stick to your list to avoid impulse purchases.

2. Shop Smart

Take advantage of discounts and sales, but be mindful of buying items just because they're on sale. Buy in bulk for non-perishable items, but consider the shelf life and storage space for perishables.

3. Choose Fresh and Seasonal

Opt for fresh, seasonal produce as it's often cheaper and more flavorful. Seasonal items are more likely to be on sale, helping you save money while enjoying quality ingredients.

4. Read Labels

Check the nutritional labels and ingredients of packaged items. Select products with fewer additives and preservatives to promote healthier eating.

Meal planning and grocery shopping are essential skills for anyone looking to manage their time, budget, and health effectively. By taking the time to plan your meals and shop thoughtfully, you can enjoy the benefits of saving time and money, reducing food waste, and eating more healthfully. These practices are not only a recipe for success but also a recipe for a more balanced and sustainable lifestyle.

4.2 Transportation Alternatives

During times of economic recession, individuals and communities often find themselves facing financial constraints that necessitate a reevaluation of their spending habits. One area where such adjustments can be particularly impactful is transportation. The cost of owning and operating a personal vehicle, along with the expenses associated with public transportation, can strain the budgets of many households when money is tight. In this context, exploring transportation alternatives becomes not only a financial necessity but also an opportunity to contribute to sustainability and reduce the overall economic burden.

1. Carpooling and Ridesharing:

Carpooling and ridesharing are excellent alternatives to reduce transportation costs. These options allow individuals to share the expenses of fuel, maintenance, and parking. Online platforms and mobile apps have made it easier than ever to find others with similar commuting routes or transportation needs. By carpooling, not only can you cut down on expenses, but you also reduce the number of vehicles on the road, which is environmentally beneficial.

2. Public Transportation: Public transportation remains a cost-effective option during a recession. Buses, subways, trams, and commuter trains offer a lower-cost alternative to owning and maintaining a personal vehicle. Many cities offer reduced fares for seniors, students, and low-income individuals, making it accessible to a broader population.

3. Cycling: Cycling is not only an environmentally friendly mode of transportation but also an

economical one. During a recession, investing in a bicycle can be a smart choice. It's a one-time expense, and maintenance costs are minimal. Cities are increasingly investing in bike lanes and infrastructure to promote cycling as a viable commuting option.

4. Walking: While not always feasible for long commutes, walking is a free and healthy mode of transportation for short distances. It can save you money on fuel and public transport fares, and it's an excellent way to

stay active.

5. Telecommuting: Remote work has become more prevalent, especially in response to the COVID-19 pandemic. If your job allows it, telecommuting can be a significant cost-saving option. You can eliminate commuting expenses entirely, from fuel and public transport to parking fees.

6. Shared Mobility Services: The sharing economy has introduced various mobility services, such as bike-sharing, scooter-sharing, and

car-sharing programs. These services offer cost-effective transportation options for short trips without the commitment of owning a vehicle.

7. Local Community Initiatives: During a recession, communities often come together to address common challenges. Consider joining or initiating a community carpool, shuttle service, or ride-sharing program. These local initiatives can be tailored to your community's specific needs and can

provide affordable transportation options.

8. Financial Assistance Programs: Government and nonprofit organizations sometimes offer financial assistance programs to help low-income individuals and families access transportation. These programs can include subsidies for public transportation, reduced-fare programs, and even vehicle purchase assistance for those in need.

9. Alternative Fuels: If you need to

drive, consider using alternative fuels like natural gas or electricity, which can be more cost-effective and environmentally friendly in the long run. Electric vehicles (EVs) are becoming increasingly accessible and often have lower operating costs than traditional gasoline-powered cars.

10. Budgeting and Financial Planning: Regardless of the mode of transportation you choose, effective budgeting and financial planning are crucial during a recession.

Tracking your transportation expenses and seeking opportunities to cut costs can help you navigate economic challenges.

When a recession places a strain on personal finances, transportation alternatives can provide significant relief. These alternatives not only help individuals save money but also contribute to reducing environmental impact and improving overall well-being. By exploring these options and adapting to changing economic conditions, individuals and communities can weather financial hardships more effectively.

Chapter 5

Increasing Your Income

5.1 Exploring Additional Income Streams

Diversify Your Financial Portfolio.

In an era where financial stability is a top priority, the concept of exploring additional income streams has gained tremendous popularity. People are increasingly recognizing the importance of diversifying their financial portfolios to secure their future and create a safety net in case of unexpected circumstances. This article delves into the significance of diversification, various income-generating avenues, and the steps to effectively explore additional income streams.

The Importance of Diversification

Diversification is a fundamental principle in finance. It involves spreading your investments and income sources across a range of assets to reduce risk. In the context of personal finance, diversification means not relying solely on a single income source, such as a full-time job. Instead, it's about creating a mosaic of income streams, which can provide stability and financial security.

There are several reasons why diversifying your income sources is essential:

1. Risk Mitigation: Relying on a single income source exposes you to greater risk. Job losses, economic downturns, or industry-specific

challenges can have a significant impact on your financial stability. Diversification minimizes this risk.

2. Income Stability: Multiple income streams can provide a stable and consistent cash flow. Even if one source experiences fluctuations or setbacks, the others can help fill the gap.

3. Financial Independence: Building multiple income streams can help you become less dependent on a single employer, giving you greater control over your financial destiny.

4. Achieving Financial Goals: Additional income streams can accelerate your progress toward achieving various financial goals, such as buying a home, saving for retirement, or starting a business.

Exploring Various Income Streams

There are numerous income-generating avenues to consider when diversifying your financial portfolio. Here are some common ones:

1. Side Hustles: Many individuals

engage in side hustles or part-time work to supplement their primary income. These can include freelance work, gig economy jobs, consulting, or selling products online.

2. Investments: Investing in stocks, bonds, mutual funds, real estate, or starting a small business can provide passive income. While these carry risk, they can also yield substantial rewards.

3. Rental Income: Owning rental properties and leasing them to tenants is a classic way to generate

consistent monthly income.

4. Dividend Stocks: Investing in dividend-paying stocks allows you to earn a portion of a company's profits regularly.

5. Online Income: The internet offers various opportunities to earn, such as blogging, affiliate marketing, YouTube channels, or selling digital products.

6. Passive Income Streams: Creating assets like e-books, apps, or YouTube videos that continue to

generate income with minimal ongoing effort.

7. Peer-to-Peer Lending: Participating in peer-to-peer lending platforms can offer attractive interest rates and monthly returns.

8. Teaching and Coaching: Sharing your expertise by offering courses, tutoring, or coaching services can be a lucrative way to diversify your income.

Steps to Effectively Explore Additional Income Streams

1. Set Clear Goals: Begin by defining your financial goals and understanding why you want to diversify your income. Are you looking for financial security, a new career path, or to fund a specific project?

2. Assess Your Skills and Interests: Identify your skills, passions, and areas of expertise. This will help you choose income streams that align with your strengths.

3. Research and Education: Invest time in researching potential

income streams. Read books, take online courses, and network with individuals already successful in those areas.

4. Create a Plan: Develop a strategic plan that outlines how you will pursue and manage each income stream. This should include financial projections, time commitments, and resources needed.

5. Start Small: Don't overwhelm yourself by attempting too many income streams simultaneously. Begin with one or two and expand as

you gain experience and confidence.

6. Dedicate Time and Effort: Building additional income streams takes time and effort. Be prepared to balance your primary job and new ventures, at least initially.

7. Track and Adjust: Continually monitor the performance of your income streams. Adjust your strategies as needed to maximize profitability and efficiency.

8. Manage Finances Wisely: Keep personal and business finances

separate. Create a budget and adhere to it to ensure that your additional income streams contribute positively to your overall financial health.

Actually, exploring additional income streams is a wise and prudent financial strategy. Diversifying your income can provide a safety net, increase your financial stability, and help you achieve your long-term goals. Whether you choose to start a side hustle, invest, or monetize your skills online, the key is to approach it with dedication, perseverance, and a well-thought-out plan. Remember, the journey towards financial diversification may be challenging, but the rewards can be significant and life-changing.

5.2 Freelancing and Gig Work

Freelancing and Gig Work in Recession: Navigating the New Normal

In times of economic uncertainty, recessions, and global crises, the world of work undergoes significant transformations. One of the most notable shifts has been the growing prominence of freelancing and gig work as an alternative and adaptable employment option. The COVID-19 pandemic, which began in 2019, further accelerated this trend. Here, we will explore the dynamics of freelancing and gig work during a recession, including the advantages and challenges, and offer insights into how both workers and businesses can navigate this evolving landscape.

The Rise of Freelancing and Gig Work

The freelance and gig economy has been on the rise for years, driven by factors such as technological advancements, changing labor preferences, and the pursuit of a more flexible work-life balance. However, the onset of a recession often intensifies this trend for several reasons.

1. Economic Uncertainty: During a

recession, traditional job security wanes, and many employers become hesitant to hire full-time employees. As a result, workers turn to freelancing and gig work to maintain income stability.

2. Cost Efficiency: Businesses seek cost-effective solutions during recessions, and hiring freelancers can be more cost-efficient than hiring full-time employees who require benefits and long-term commitments.

3. Skills and Expertise: Freelancers

often bring specialized skills and expertise to the table, making them highly sought after during a recession, when businesses need to adapt to changing market demands quickly.

Advantages of Freelancing and Gig Work in a Recession

1. Flexibility: Freelancers have the flexibility to choose when, where, and how they work, allowing them to adapt to the changing economic landscape.

2. Diverse Income Streams: Gig workers can diversify their income by taking on various projects for different clients, which can help buffer the impact of economic downturns.

3. Quick Adaption: Freelancers can quickly pivot to new opportunities and markets, enabling them to adjust to shifts in demand and industry requirements.

4. Remote Work: The rise of remote work has expanded the pool of available freelance opportunities,

enabling workers to access a global client base.

5. Self-Reliance: Freelancers have the autonomy to manage their own careers, making them less vulnerable to layoffs and corporate restructuring.

Challenges of Freelancing and Gig Work in a Recession

While freelancing and gig work offer numerous advantages, there are also inherent challenges, especially in a recession.

1. Income Inconsistency: Freelancers often face fluctuations in income, as they are paid per project or gig, making it challenging to predict financial stability.

2. Lack of Benefits: Freelancers typically do not receive traditional employee benefits such as health insurance, retirement plans, or paid leave.

3. Competition: The gig economy can be highly competitive, with a large pool of workers vying for the same opportunities, which can drive

down prices and job availability.

4. Financial Responsibility: Freelancers must manage their own taxes, expenses, and retirement planning, which can be overwhelming for those new to the freelance world.

Navigating Freelancing and Gig Work in a Recession

For both workers and businesses, navigating the world of freelancing and gig work during a recession requires careful planning and adaptation:

For Workers:

1. Diversify Your Skills: Acquire a broad range of skills to increase your marketability in various industries.

2. Build a Financial Safety Net: Save for emergencies and consider investing in insurance and retirement plans.

3. Network Actively: Build a strong network to find new opportunities and long-term clients.

4. Stay Informed: Keep a close eye

on industry trends and adapt accordingly.

For Businesses:

1. Embrace Flexible Talent: Consider hiring freelancers for specific projects or tasks to reduce overhead costs.

2. Develop Clear Contracts: Create transparent agreements with freelancers to ensure expectations are met.

3. Invest in Training: Provide opportunities for freelancers to

upskill and stay relevant in the workforce.

4. Promote Inclusivity: Ensure diversity and inclusion within your freelancing network to tap into a broader range of talents.

Freelancing and gig work have become integral components of the modern workforce, especially during times of economic recession. While these working arrangements offer significant advantages, workers and businesses must also confront challenges related to income stability, benefits, and competition. By understanding the dynamics and adapting accordingly, freelancers and organizations can harness the flexibility and expertise that this evolving employment landscape offers, ensuring resilience and sustainability in an uncertain economic environment.

5.3 Online Learning and Skills Enhancement

The COVID-19 pandemic and its economic repercussions have brought about significant changes in the way people work, learn, and adapt to the ever-evolving job market. As businesses faced disruptions and layoffs became commonplace, individuals were left with the stark realization that skills enhancement is a key factor in not only surviving but thriving during a recession. This realization has led to a surge in online learning, creating a powerful synergy between education and economic resilience.

The Shift to Online Learning

The digital revolution had already

begun transforming education prior to the pandemic, but the abrupt shift to remote work and learning in 2020 accelerated this transition. Online learning platforms, from massive open online courses (MOOCs) to specialized platforms like Coursera, Udemy, and edX, experienced exponential growth. The advantages of online learning became increasingly apparent, making it the go-to option for upskilling and reskilling.

1. Accessibility: Online courses can

be accessed from anywhere, leveling the playing field for people in remote areas or regions with limited educational resources.

2. Flexibility: The asynchronous nature of online learning allows individuals to learn at their own pace and on their own schedule, making it easier for those juggling work, family, and other commitments.

3. Affordability: Online courses are often more cost-effective than traditional education. Many

platforms offer free courses, while paid ones are still considerably more affordable than attending a brick-and-mortar institution.

4. Diversity of Courses: Online platforms offer a vast array of courses, from coding and digital marketing to soft skills like communication and leadership. This diversity caters to the needs of a wide range of learners.

The Role of Online Learning in Skill Enhancement

Online learning has become a lifeline for individuals looking to enhance their skills during a recession. Here's how it plays a crucial role:

1. Skills Diversification: In an economic downturn, many professions become obsolete or experience a sharp decline in demand. Online learning allows individuals to diversify their skill set, making them more adaptable to changing job markets.

2. Skill Relevance: The dynamic

nature of online courses ensures that learners can access the most up-to-date information and trends in their field, ensuring their skills remain relevant.

3. Career Switching: For those who have lost their jobs in hard-hit sectors, online courses provide the opportunity to switch careers. They can learn new skills that are in demand, even in a recession.

4. Entrepreneurship: Online learning empowers aspiring entrepreneurs to develop business acumen,

marketing skills, and more. These skills are critical for starting and running a business, which can be a viable option during economic uncertainty.

5. Soft Skills: Besides technical skills, online courses also emphasize the development of soft skills such as communication, problem-solving, and adaptability. These skills are invaluable in any job market.

Employers and Online Learning

Employers are increasingly

recognizing the value of online learning for their workforce. Here's how they are leveraging online education during a recession:

1. Professional Development: Employers are encouraging their employees to take online courses to improve their job performance and readiness for changing roles.

2. Cost-Efficiency: Online learning can be more cost-effective for employers than traditional in-person training programs, making it an attractive option in lean

economic times.

3. Remote Work Skills: As remote work becomes more prevalent, employers are supporting their staff in acquiring the necessary skills for remote collaboration, time management, and digital communication.

Challenges and Considerations

While online learning has become a vital tool for skills enhancement in a recession, it is not without its challenges and considerations:

1. Digital Divide: Not everyone has equal access to the internet and devices. This digital divide can hinder the opportunities for some individuals.

2. Quality Assurance: The quality of online courses can vary. Learners need to do their due diligence to choose reputable platforms and courses.

3. Self-Discipline: Online learning requires self-discipline and time management. Not everyone is suited for this style of learning.

4. Credential Recognition: Some employers may not fully recognize online credentials, and learners may need to work harder to prove the value of their online education.

In an era of economic instability and rapid technological change, online learning is an essential component of skills enhancement. It offers accessibility, flexibility, and affordability, enabling individuals to adapt to the evolving job market. Employers, too, are embracing online learning to develop their workforce's skills. While challenges exist, online learning has proved to be a powerful tool for individuals and organizations navigating the uncertainties of a recession. As we move forward, it is clear that online education will continue to play a pivotal role in building a resilient and adaptable workforce.

Chapter 6

Debt Management

6.1 Addressing High-Interest Debt

High-interest debt can be a significant burden, often causing stress, financial strain, and impeding your ability to achieve your financial goals. Whether it's credit card debt, personal loans, or other high-interest obligations, it's essential to take proactive steps to address and manage it effectively. In this comprehensive guide, we will explore various strategies and tips to help you tackle high-interest debt and regain control of your financial future.

Understanding High-Interest Debt

Before delving into strategies for addressing high-interest debt, it's crucial to understand what it is and why it can be detrimental to your financial well-being. High-interest debt typically refers to loans or credit card balances with annual interest rates significantly above the average. These high rates mean that you're paying a substantial amount of money just in interest, making it challenging to make headway in reducing the principal balance.

Common sources of high-interest debt include:

1. Credit Cards: Credit cards often have some of the highest interest rates in the consumer lending industry. It's not uncommon for credit card APRs to exceed 20%, and if you carry a balance, the interest charges can accumulate rapidly.

2. Payday Loans: These short-term, high-interest loans are notorious for their exorbitant interest rates, trapping borrowers in a cycle of debt.

3. Personal Loans: While personal loans can serve as a helpful financial tool, some unsecured personal loans come with high interest rates, particularly for individuals with lower credit scores.

4. Medical Bills: Medical debt can also be a source of high-interest debt if it accumulates interest over time, especially if you are unable to

pay the full amount immediately.

5. Auto Title Loans: Similar to payday loans, auto title loans often carry substantial interest rates, and they are secured by your vehicle, posing a significant risk if you cannot repay the loan.

Strategies for Addressing High-Interest Debt

1. Create a Detailed Budget: The first step in addressing high-interest debt is to create a comprehensive budget. List all your sources of income and

all your expenses. This will help you identify areas where you can cut back and allocate more money toward debt repayment.

2. Prioritize High-Interest Debts: Make a list of all your debts, arranging them in order of interest rate, with the highest interest debt at the top. Focus on paying off the high-interest debts first, as they cost you the most over time.

3. Negotiate Lower Interest Rates: Contact your creditors and attempt to negotiate lower interest rates,

especially if you have a good payment history. Credit card companies may be willing to reduce your interest rate to retain your business.

4. Consider Debt Consolidation: Debt consolidation involves taking out a new loan, often with a lower interest rate, to pay off your high-interest debts. This can simplify your payments and potentially save you money.

5. Debt Snowball or Avalanche Method: These methods involve

systematically paying off debts. With the snowball method, you pay off the smallest debts first to build momentum, while the avalanche method focuses on high-interest debts to save on interest costs.

6. Increase Income: Look for opportunities to increase your income, such as a part-time job, freelancing, or selling unused assets. The additional income can be directed towards debt repayment.

7. Cut Unnecessary Expenses: Examine your spending habits and

identify areas where you can cut back. This might mean reducing dining out, canceling subscription services, or finding more cost-effective ways to meet your needs.

8. Emergency Fund: While it may seem counterintuitive to save money while you have high-interest debt, having a small emergency fund can prevent you from going deeper into debt when unexpected expenses arise.

9. Seek Professional Help: If you're overwhelmed by your debt, consider

reaching out to a credit counseling agency or a financial advisor for guidance and debt management programs.

10. Avoid Accruing More Debt: While you work on paying off high-interest debt, refrain from accumulating new debt. This means using your credit cards sparingly and responsibly.

The Emotional Side of High-Interest Debt

High-interest debt isn't just a financial problem; it can also take an emotional toll. The stress and anxiety associated with debt can affect your overall well-being. It's essential to stay positive and patient throughout your debt repayment journey. Remember that addressing high-interest debt is a process that may take time, but the long-term financial freedom is worth the effort.

Addressing high-interest debt is a critical step towards achieving financial stability and security. By understanding the nature of high-interest debt, creating a solid plan, and implementing effective strategies, you can take control of your financial future. Remember that there is no one-size-fits-all solution, and it may take time and discipline to become debt-free. The key is to stay committed to your financial goals and make informed decisions about managing your debt.

6.2 Loan Refinancing

Loan refinancing is a financial strategy that involves replacing an existing loan with a new one that typically offers better terms, such as lower interest rates or extended repayment periods. This process is commonly utilized for various types of loans, including mortgages, auto loans, and student loans, and it can provide several benefits to borrowers. In this comprehensive discussion, we will delve into the concept of loan refinancing, its potential advantages, the different types of loans that can be refinanced, and the steps involved in the refinancing process.

Understanding Loan Refinancing

Loan refinancing, also known as loan consolidation or loan restructuring, is a financial maneuver used to modify the terms of an existing loan in a way that is more favorable to the borrower. This is typically done to reduce the financial burden associated with the loan by securing a lower interest rate, lowering monthly payments, or extending the loan's repayment term. The decision to refinance a loan is influenced by the prevailing economic conditions, the borrower's creditworthiness, and the borrower's long-term financial goals.

Types of Loans That Can Be Refinanced

1. Mortgage Refinancing: Mortgage refinancing is one of the most common forms of loan refinancing. Homeowners opt for this when they can secure a mortgage with a lower interest rate, which can lead to significant long-term savings. It can also be used to switch from an adjustable-rate mortgage (ARM) to a fixed-rate mortgage to provide

stability in monthly payments.

2. Auto Loan Refinancing: Borrowers with high-interest auto loans can refinance their loans to obtain better interest rates and potentially lower their monthly car payments. This is especially useful if their creditworthiness has improved since they initially obtained the loan.

3. Student Loan Refinancing: Student loan refinancing is employed to replace existing student loans with a new one featuring more favorable terms. This

can help graduates save money on interest and, in some cases, reduce the monthly payments. Federal student loans can be refinanced privately, but this may result in the loss of certain benefits and protections.

4. Personal Loan Refinancing: Personal loans are often used for a variety of purposes, and refinancing may be an option to secure a lower interest rate, which can lead to cost savings. However, personal loan refinancing is less common

compared to other types of loans.

5. Business Loan Refinancing: Entrepreneurs and business owners can also refinance their existing business loans. This can be advantageous if they can obtain more favorable terms, such as lower interest rates, longer repayment periods, or access to additional capital.

Benefits of Loan Refinancing

The primary advantages of loan refinancing include:

1. Reduced Monthly Payments: By securing a lower interest rate, borrowers can reduce their monthly payments, making it easier to manage their financial obligations.

2. Interest Savings: Refinancing can result in significant savings over the life of the loan, especially for long-term loans like mortgages.

3. Debt Consolidation: Multiple loans can be consolidated into a single loan with better terms, simplifying the borrower's financial situation.

4. Improved Credit Score: Timely payments on a refinanced loan can positively impact the borrower's credit score.

5. Flexible Repayment Terms: Borrowers can choose from various repayment options, such as fixed-rate or adjustable-rate loans, and may be able to extend the loan term to reduce the monthly payment.

The Refinancing Process

The loan refinancing process typically involves the following steps:

1. Assessment: The borrower should assess their current loan terms, creditworthiness, and financial goals to determine whether refinancing is a viable option.

2. Credit Check: Lenders will conduct a credit check to evaluate the borrower's creditworthiness. A good credit score can result in more favorable loan terms.

3. Shop for Lenders: Borrowers should research and compare different lenders to find the best refinancing offers. This involves

considering interest rates, fees, and terms.

4. Application: The borrower submits a loan application to the chosen lender, which typically includes providing financial documentation.

5. Approval and Closing: Once approved, the borrower will review the new loan terms and sign the necessary paperwork. The new loan pays off the existing loan, and the refinancing process is complete.

Considerations and Cautions

While loan refinancing can offer numerous benefits, there are certain considerations and cautions to keep in mind:

- Fees: Refinancing often involves fees, such as application fees, closing costs, and appraisal fees. These expenses should be factored into the decision.

- Lost Benefits: Refinancing federal student loans into private loans may result in the loss of federal loan protections, such as income-driven repayment plans and loan forgiveness options.

- Credit Impact: Multiple loan applications can temporarily lower the borrower's credit score, so it's essential to be selective when shopping for lenders.

- Long-Term Costs: Extending the loan term to reduce monthly payments may lead to higher total interest costs over time.

- Market Conditions: Interest rates

and economic conditions play a crucial role in determining the benefits of loan refinancing. Borrowers should monitor these factors.

Loan refinancing is a financial strategy that allows borrowers to modify the terms of their existing loans to their advantage. Whether it's a mortgage, auto loan, student loan, personal loan, or business loan, the decision to refinance should be made after careful consideration of current financial circumstances and long-term goals. By following the appropriate steps and being mindful of potential drawbacks, borrowers can make informed decisions that lead to better financial outcomes.

6.3 Debt Consolidation

Debt consolidation is a financial strategy that many individuals and families consider when they find themselves burdened by multiple debts. It's a method aimed at simplifying your financial life by combining several outstanding debts into a single, more manageable one. While this may sound like an attractive solution, it's essential to understand the intricacies of debt consolidation before deciding if it's the right choice for your financial situation.

Debt consolidation is the process of taking out a new loan to pay off existing debts. The primary goal is to reduce the number of monthly payments and potentially secure a lower interest rate, which can lead to more manageable monthly payments. There are several ways to consolidate debt, and the method you choose depends on your individual circumstances and the types of debt you have.

Different Methods of Debt Consolidation

1. Debt Consolidation Loans: This is one of the most common methods of consolidating debt. You apply for a personal loan, usually with a fixed interest rate, and use the funds to pay off your existing debts. By doing so, you replace multiple creditors with a single lender.

2. Balance Transfer Credit Cards: Some credit card companies offer balance transfer cards with low or 0% introductory APR (annual percentage rate) for a specified period. You can transfer your existing credit card balances to this new card, giving you time to pay off the debt interest-free. However, it's important to pay attention to balance transfer fees and the regular APR once the introductory period ends.

3. Home Equity Loans or HELOCs: If

you're a homeowner, you might consider using the equity in your home to consolidate debt. Home equity loans and home equity lines of credit (HELOCs) can offer lower interest rates than other types of loans because they are secured by your property.

4. Debt Management Plans: Non-profit credit counseling agencies offer debt management plans (DMPs). They work with your creditors to lower interest rates and consolidate your unsecured debts

into a single monthly payment. This method can be effective if you have high credit card debts.

5. Debt Consolidation Companies: There are for-profit debt consolidation companies that offer services to negotiate with your creditors and consolidate your debts into one monthly payment. Be cautious and do thorough research before choosing this option, as there are both reputable and unscrupulous companies in this industry.

Pros of Debt Consolidation

1. Simplified Finances: Debt consolidation simplifies your financial life by reducing multiple payments to just one.

2. Lower Interest Rates: If you qualify for a lower interest rate on your consolidation loan, you can potentially save money on interest payments.

3. Fixed Payments: Many consolidation loans offer fixed monthly payments, making it easier

to budget and plan for your financial future.

Cons of Debt Consolidation

1. Potential for More Debt: Debt consolidation doesn't eliminate your debt but simply restructures it. Some people may fall into the trap of accumulating more debt after consolidating their existing obligations.

2. Interest Costs: While a lower interest rate is a potential benefit, it's not guaranteed. You could end

up paying more in interest over the life of the new loan.

3. Risk of Collateral: If you use your home as collateral, you risk losing it if you can't make payments on the consolidation loan.

4. Credit Score Impact: The process of obtaining a new loan can temporarily impact your credit score, but responsible management of the consolidation loan can help rebuild it over time.

Is Debt Consolidation Right for You?

Debt consolidation can be a helpful strategy for individuals who are committed to managing their finances wisely. It's crucial to weigh the pros and cons carefully and, if necessary, consult with a financial advisor. Consider your current credit score, the interest rates you're eligible for, and your ability to make consistent payments.

Before pursuing debt consolidation, it's also essential to address the root causes of your debt. If overspending, poor budgeting, or other financial habits contributed to your debt, make sure you've taken steps to address these issues to prevent a recurring cycle of indebtedness.

Debt consolidation can be a valuable tool for regaining control of your financial situation, but it's not a one-size-fits-all solution. Be sure to research your options, carefully evaluate your financial standing, and make an informed decision based on your specific circumstances.

Chapter 7

Savings and Investments

7.1 Building an Emergency Fund

An emergency fund is like a financial safety net, providing you with peace of mind and a sense of security in times of unexpected crises. It's a critical component of sound financial planning and can make the difference between minor inconveniences and major financial setbacks. In this comprehensive guide, we'll explore the importance of building an emergency fund, how to get started, and the best practices to maintain it.

The Importance of an Emergency Fund

1. Financial Protection: Life is full of surprises, and not all of them are pleasant. From medical emergencies to sudden job loss or unexpected car repairs, having an emergency fund can be a lifesaver. It prevents you from resorting to high-interest loans, selling assets, or

going into debt to deal with these unforeseen situations.

2. Reduced Stress: Financial stress can take a toll on your mental and physical health. An emergency fund provides a buffer, reducing anxiety and ensuring you have the means to handle unexpected expenses with confidence.

3. Long-Term Financial Goals: Without an emergency fund, any unplanned expense can set you back on your financial goals, such as saving for a down payment on a

house, funding your children's education, or retiring comfortably. With a well-funded emergency fund, you can continue working towards these goals even when life throws you a curveball.

How to Build an Emergency Fund

1. Set a Goal: Determine how much you want to save in your emergency fund. Financial experts typically recommend saving at least 3 to 6 months' worth of living expenses. However, your specific goal should consider your individual

circumstances, such as family size, income, and job stability.

2. Open a Dedicated Account: To ensure your emergency fund remains separate from your regular spending accounts, consider opening a separate savings account. This will also make it harder to dip into the fund for non-emergencies.

3. Create a Budget: Assess your monthly income and expenses to identify how much you can realistically set aside for your emergency fund. Allocate a fixed

amount each month, making it a non-negotiable part of your budget.

4. Automate Your Savings: To make saving easier, set up an automatic transfer from your primary checking account to your emergency fund account. This ensures you consistently contribute to your fund without thinking about it.

5. Use Windfalls and Bonuses: Any unexpected windfalls, such as tax refunds, work bonuses, or unexpected gifts, can be a significant boost to your emergency

fund. Consider allocating a portion of these funds to your safety net.

Maintaining Your Emergency Fund

1. Regularly Review and Adjust: Life circumstances change, and so should your emergency fund goal. Review it periodically and adjust if necessary. For instance, if you get a higher-paying job, you might consider increasing your emergency fund target.

2. Avoid Temptation: It can be tempting to dip into your emergency

fund for non-urgent expenses. Remember that it's there to protect you during true emergencies, such as medical bills or urgent home repairs. Stick to your budget and other savings goals for less pressing financial needs.

3. Replenish After Use: If you do have to use your emergency fund, make it a priority to replenish the amount you withdrew as soon as your financial situation stabilizes. This will ensure that your fund is always ready for the next unexpected event.

4. Consider Investments: As your emergency fund grows beyond your target, consider investing a portion of it in low-risk, easily accessible investments like a money market account. This can help your fund keep pace with inflation and potentially yield better returns while still being readily available when needed.

Building and maintaining an emergency fund is a fundamental pillar of personal finance. It offers protection, peace of mind, and the ability to stay on course with your long-term financial goals. With careful planning, discipline, and determination, you can create a financial safety net that will help you weather life's storms and emerge financially secure. Remember, it's not a matter of "if" an emergency will occur, but "when," so start building your emergency fund today.

7.2 Smart Investment Strategies

Smart investment strategies are essential for individuals looking to grow their wealth, achieve financial goals, and secure their financial future. Whether you're a seasoned investor or a novice, having a well-thought-out investment plan can make a significant difference in your financial success. In this article, we'll explore some key principles and strategies for making smart investments.

1. Diversification:

One of the fundamental principles of smart investing is diversification. This strategy involves spreading your investments across different asset classes, such as stocks, bonds, real estate, and commodities. Diversification helps reduce risk because if one asset class underperforms, the others may compensate. It's often said, "Don't put all your eggs in one basket."

2. Risk Tolerance:

Understanding your risk tolerance is crucial when developing an investment strategy. Your risk tolerance is influenced by factors such as your age, financial goals, and how comfortable you are with market fluctuations. Younger investors with a longer time horizon can generally afford to take more risks, while those nearing retirement may prefer more conservative investments.

3. Investment Goals:

Clearly define your investment goals. Are you saving for retirement, a down payment on a house, or your child's education? Knowing your objectives will help you determine the appropriate investment horizon, risk level, and asset allocation.

4. Asset Allocation:

Asset allocation involves deciding how to distribute your investments among different asset classes. Your asset allocation should align with your risk tolerance and financial goals. For example, a typical allocation for a long-term investor might be 60% stocks and 40% bonds.

5. Dollar-Cost Averaging:

Dollar-cost averaging is a strategy where you invest a fixed amount of money at regular intervals, regardless of market conditions. This approach can help reduce the impact of market volatility and emotions on your investment decisions.

6. Research and Due Diligence:

Before investing in any asset, conduct thorough research and due diligence. Understand the companies you're investing in, the industries they operate in, and the economic factors that may affect their performance. Additionally, research historical market trends to make informed decisions.

7. Long-Term Perspective:

Successful investors often have a long-term perspective. They understand that short-term market fluctuations are common and can be unpredictable. Avoid making impulsive decisions based on daily or weekly market movements.

8. Avoid Market Timing:

Market timing, the act of trying to predict when to buy or sell investments based on short-term market movements, is a risky strategy. Very few investors consistently succeed with market timing. Instead, focus on a long-term investment approach.

9. Review and Adjust:

Regularly review your investment portfolio to ensure it remains aligned with your goals and risk tolerance. Rebalancing your portfolio by selling overperforming assets and buying underperforming ones can help maintain your desired asset allocation.

10. Seek Professional Advice:

If you're uncertain about investment strategies or don't have the time or expertise to manage your investments, consider consulting a financial advisor. They can provide guidance, recommend suitable investment options, and help you make informed decisions.

11. Consider Tax Efficiency:

Tax-efficient investing can significantly impact your returns. Look for tax-advantaged accounts such as IRAs and 401(k)s, and consider tax-efficient investment strategies like holding investments for the long term to qualify for lower capital gains tax rates.

12. Stay Informed:

Stay informed about economic and market developments. This knowledge can help you make well-informed investment decisions. Reading financial news, following reputable sources, and staying aware of geopolitical events can be valuable.

Smart investment strategies are crucial for building and preserving wealth. Whether you're a conservative or aggressive investor, the key is to have a well-thought-out plan that aligns with your goals and risk tolerance. By diversifying your portfolio, understanding your risk tolerance, and adhering to a long-term perspective, you can increase your chances of financial success. Always remember that investing involves risk, and there are no guarantees, so it's essential to be well-prepared and informed.

Chapter 8

Maintaining a Healthy Mindset

8.1 Dealing with Financial Stress

Financial stress is a common and significant source of anxiety for many individuals and families. It can be caused by various factors, including job loss, unexpected medical expenses, high levels of debt, or simply living paycheck to paycheck. While it's natural to feel stressed when facing financial challenges, managing this stress is essential for your overall well-being. In this article, we'll explore strategies and tips to help you deal with financial stress and regain control of your financial situation.

1. Assess Your Financial Situation:

The first step in addressing financial stress is to have a clear understanding of your financial situation. Create a comprehensive budget that outlines your income, expenses, and debts. This will help you identify areas where you can make changes and cut costs.

2. Prioritize Your Expenses:

Once you have a budget in place, prioritize your expenses. Ensure that you cover essentials such as housing, utilities, groceries, and debt payments before spending on non-essential items. Consider creating an emergency fund to help you deal with unexpected expenses without resorting to more debt.

3. Set Realistic Financial Goals:

Having clear financial goals can

help motivate you and provide a sense of purpose. Whether it's paying off debt, saving for retirement, or buying a house, setting achievable goals can give you a sense of control over your financial future.

4. Seek Professional Help:

If your financial situation is overwhelming, don't hesitate to seek professional assistance. Financial advisors or credit counselors can provide guidance and support in managing your finances and creating a debt repayment plan.

5. Develop a Debt Repayment Strategy:

High levels of debt can be a significant source of financial stress. Develop a strategy for paying off your debts, starting with high-interest debts. Consider debt consolidation or negotiating with creditors to reduce interest rates or create more manageable payment plans.

6. Increase Your Financial Literacy:

Knowledge is power when it comes to managing finances. Educate yourself about personal finance, budgeting, and investing. There are plenty of free resources available online, and community courses can also help improve your financial literacy.

7. Adopt a Frugal Lifestyle:

Temporarily adopting a frugal lifestyle can help alleviate financial stress. Cut back on non-essential expenses, look for discounts and coupons, and explore cost-effective alternatives for your daily needs.

8. Increase Your Income:

If possible, explore opportunities to increase your income. This might involve asking for a raise, finding a part-time job, freelancing, or starting a side business. Increasing your income can provide a significant financial buffer.

9. Manage Your Emotions:

Financial stress can take a toll on

your emotional well-being. It's crucial to find healthy ways to cope with these emotions. Exercise, meditation, and talking to friends or a therapist can be effective ways to manage stress.

10. Avoid Unhealthy Coping Mechanisms:

Avoid turning to unhealthy coping mechanisms like excessive drinking or gambling, as these can exacerbate financial problems and emotional distress.

11. Stay Positive and Patient:

Dealing with financial stress can be a long and challenging journey. Stay positive, patient, and persistent. Understand that it takes time to improve your financial situation.

12. Build a Support System:

Don't go through financial stress alone. Lean on your friends and family for emotional support, and consider joining support groups or online communities where people share similar financial struggles.

13. Monitor Your Progress:

Regularly review your financial situation and track your progress. Celebrate small victories, and adjust your financial plan as needed.

14. Consider Professional Help for Mental Health:

If financial stress is severely affecting your mental health, consider seeking professional help from a therapist or counselor who can provide guidance on coping with anxiety and stress.

Dealing with financial stress is not an overnight process, but with determination and the right strategies, you can regain control of your financial situation and reduce the stress it causes. Remember that you are not alone, and there are resources and people available to support you in your journey to financial well-being.

8.2 Staying Informed but Not Panicking

Staying Informed but Not Panicking in Finance: A Guide to Financial

Resilience

In the fast-paced world of finance, staying informed is crucial for making sound investment decisions and protecting your financial well-being. However, it's equally important not to succumb to panic when faced with market volatility, economic uncertainties, or financial crises. This delicate balance requires a combination of knowledge, emotional control, and a well-thought-out financial strategy.

1. Understand the Basics:

Before diving into complex financial instruments or investing strategies, it's essential to have a solid understanding of the fundamentals. Familiarize yourself with key financial concepts such as stocks, bonds, mutual funds, and diversification. Knowing the basics can help you make more informed decisions and reduce the likelihood of making hasty choices.

2. Continuous Learning:

Finance is an ever-evolving field. Stay informed by reading reputable financial news sources, following market trends, and understanding economic indicators. Consider enrolling in courses or seminars to enhance your financial literacy. Learning is a lifelong process, and the more you know, the more confident you'll be in your financial decisions.

3. Diversify Your Investments:

A well-diversified portfolio can help mitigate risk. By spreading your investments across different asset classes, industries, and geographic regions, you can reduce the impact of a downturn in any single sector. Diversification is a key strategy for staying resilient in the face of market fluctuations.

4. Maintain a Long-Term Perspective:

Markets will always have their ups and downs. It's crucial to remember that investing is a long-term endeavor. Short-term fluctuations are often noise in the grand scheme of your financial journey. Stick to your investment plan and avoid making impulsive decisions based on temporary market movements.

5. Emergency Fund:

Having an emergency fund in place is a fundamental part of financial resilience. This safety net can help you weather unexpected expenses or financial setbacks without needing to liquidate investments during a downturn.

6. Consult with Professionals:

Consider seeking advice from financial professionals, such as financial advisors or certified planners. They can provide guidance tailored to your specific financial situation and goals. However, make sure to work with individuals who have a fiduciary duty to act in your best interest.

7. Avoid Emotional Decision-Making:

Emotional reactions can be detrimental to your financial health. Fear and greed can drive impulsive actions that may not be in your best interest. Instead, base your decisions on research, analysis, and a clear understanding of your financial objectives.

8. Set Realistic Goals:

Establish clear financial goals and regularly review them. This provides you with a roadmap for your financial journey and can help you stay on course even during turbulent times.

9. Risk Tolerance Assessment:

Understand your risk tolerance. Different individuals have different levels of comfort with risk. Your investment strategy should align with your risk tolerance to ensure that you can withstand market fluctuations without undue stress.

10. Keep an Eye on Costs:

High fees and expenses can erode your returns over time. Be mindful of the costs associated with your investments, and consider low-cost index funds and ETFs as part of your portfolio.

11. Stay Calm During Crises:

Financial crises and market crashes are part of the economic cycle. Rather than panicking, consider them as opportunities. Historically, markets have recovered from downturns. Staying calm and even investing more during a downturn can be a successful long-term strategy.

12. Regular Reassessment:

Periodically review and adjust your financial plan. Life circumstances, goals, and market conditions change over time. Being adaptable and willing to make strategic adjustments is essential for financial success.

Staying informed but not panicking in finance is a delicate art that requires a combination of education, emotional control, and strategic planning. By understanding the fundamentals, diversifying your investments, and maintaining a long -term perspective, you can build financial resilience and navigate the challenges of the financial world with confidence. Remember, it's not about timing the market but rather time in the market that ultimately leads to financial success.

8.3 Seeking Professional Help

In the complex world of finance, seeking professional help can be a game-changer. Whether you're an individual looking to manage your personal finances or a business aiming to navigate the financial landscape, the expertise of financial professionals can make a significant difference. This guide explores the reasons why you should consider seeking professional help in finance and the various avenues available to you.

1. Understanding the Need for Professional Help:

a. Financial Complexity: Finance is not just about balancing a checkbook; it involves intricate strategies, regulations, and market dynamics. Financial professionals are equipped to simplify this complexity.

b. Time Efficiency: Professionals can save you precious time by managing your financial matters, allowing you to focus on your core responsibilities.

2. Types of Financial Professionals:

a. Financial Planners: These experts can create comprehensive financial plans, helping you achieve your short-term and long-term financial goals.

b. Certified Public Accountants (CPAs): CPAs provide tax planning, compliance, and accounting services, ensuring you meet your tax obligations efficiently.

c. Investment Advisors: For those looking to grow their wealth, investment advisors offer guidance on investment strategies, asset allocation, and portfolio management.

d. Financial Analysts: These experts analyze financial data and market trends, aiding in making informed investment decisions.

3. Benefits of Professional Assistance:

a. Personalization: Financial

professionals tailor their advice to your specific financial situation and goals.

b. Risk Management: They can help you assess and mitigate financial risks, ensuring a secure financial future.

c. Tax Efficiency: Professionals can identify tax-saving opportunities, reducing your overall tax burden.

d. Long-Term Planning: With a professional's guidance, you can create a solid financial plan for retirement, education, or major life events.

4. Choosing the Right Professional:

a. Qualifications and Certifications: Ensure your financial professional has the necessary qualifications and is accredited by relevant organizations.

b. Fee Structure: Understand their fee structure and how they are compensated. Some professionals charge flat fees, while others work on commissions.

c. Track Record: Research their track record and client testimonials to gauge their reliability.

5. Working with a Financial Professional:

a. Open Communication: Maintain a transparent and open line of communication with your chosen professional.

b. Regular Updates: Stay informed about the progress of your financial plan and make necessary adjustments as your circumstances change.

6. Monitoring and Evaluation:

a. Periodic Reviews: Schedule regular reviews with your financial professional to ensure your financial plan remains aligned with your goals.

b. Flexibility: Be open to adjustments in your financial plan as economic conditions and personal circumstances evolve.

Seeking professional help in finance is not a sign of weakness but a smart and responsible approach to managing your financial well-being. From simplifying financial complexities to optimizing your tax situation, k professionals play a pivotal role in helping you achieve financial success. Remember, the key is to choose the right professional, maintain open communication, and adapt to changes as needed. With their guidance, you can embark on a journey towards a more secure and prosperous financial future.

Chapter 9

Long-Term Financial Resilience

9.1 Diversification and Risk Management

Diversification and risk management are fundamental concepts in the field of economics and finance. They play a crucial role in helping individuals, businesses, and even entire economies mitigate the impact of uncertainties and volatility. In this comprehensive discussion, we will explore the key principles and strategies associated with diversification and risk management in the context of the economy.

Diversification:

Diversification is the practice of spreading investments, resources, or activities across a variety of assets or areas. In the realm of economics, diversification is primarily applied to financial portfolios, industries, and income sources. The goal is to reduce risk by avoiding over-reliance on a single asset or sector. Diversification can take many forms:

1. Asset Diversification: In investment, this involves spreading funds across various asset classes, such as stocks, bonds, real estate, and commodities. The idea is that different asset classes perform differently under different economic conditions, reducing the overall risk in a portfolio.

2. Industry Diversification: Companies can diversify by operating in multiple industries. This

minimizes their vulnerability to economic downturns affecting one particular sector. For example, a conglomerate might have divisions in technology, healthcare, and energy.

3. Geographic Diversification: Expanding operations or investments across different regions or countries can protect against regional economic shocks. For instance, a multinational corporation may have subsidiaries in various countries to reduce

exposure to political or economic risks in any single nation.

4. Product Diversification: Companies can offer a variety of products or services to cater to different market segments. This approach can help maintain revenue streams during market fluctuations.

5. Income Diversification: For individuals, diversifying income sources can provide financial stability. This could involve having a part-time job, rental income, and investments in addition to a primary

source of income.

Risk Management:

Risk management is the process of identifying, assessing, and mitigating risks. In the context of the economy, risk management is crucial for stability and growth. Several risk management strategies are commonly employed:

1. Risk Assessment: Understanding the types and levels of risk is the first step. Economic risks can include market volatility, inflation, political

instability, and natural disasters. For instance, a company exporting goods internationally might face currency exchange rate risk.

2. Insurance: Businesses and individuals use insurance as a risk mitigation tool. Insurance policies can cover various risks, from property damage to health emergencies, helping to reduce financial vulnerabilities.

3. Hedging: In financial markets,

hedging is a strategy to protect against adverse price movements. For example, a company might hedge against rising commodity prices by buying futures contracts at current prices.

4. Reserves and Contingency Plans: Having financial reserves and contingency plans in place is essential. Governments often maintain foreign exchange reserves to stabilize their currency and economy during crises.

5. Regulation and Oversight:

Government regulations and oversight play a significant role in risk management. They set the rules and standards that businesses must adhere to in order to prevent systemic risks and protect consumers.

6. Scenario Analysis: Economic actors often conduct scenario analyses to anticipate and prepare for potential risks. This involves simulating various economic situations to assess their impact.

The Interplay Between

Diversification and Risk Management:

Diversification and risk management are closely intertwined. Diversification is a proactive risk management strategy that seeks to reduce exposure to specific risks, while risk management helps identify potential issues that may necessitate diversification.

The global financial crisis of 2008 is a pertinent example. Many financial institutions had concentrated their investments in mortgage-backed securities, leading to massive losses. This lack of diversification in their portfolios magnified their exposure to the risk of a housing market collapse. The subsequent market turmoil highlighted the importance of diversifying portfolios and the need for better risk management practices.

Diversification and risk management are indispensable tools for economic stability and growth. By spreading resources and investments, individuals, businesses, and economies can better weather uncertainties and economic fluctuations. Additionally, rigorous risk assessment and mitigation strategies are essential for identifying and preparing for potential risks. In an interconnected and dynamic global economy, the effective use of diversification and risk management techniques is paramount for long-term success.

9.2 Continuous Learning and Adaptation

In the fast-paced and ever-evolving

world of finance, the ability to continuously learn and adapt is not just a desirable trait; it's an absolute necessity. The financial industry is subject to constant change, influenced by factors such as economic fluctuations, technological advancements, regulatory modifications, and shifting consumer behavior. Staying competitive and relevant in this environment requires finance professionals to be committed to ongoing learning and adaptation.

1. Understanding the Need for Continuous Learning:

Finance is a field that is deeply intertwined with the global economy, and thus, it's highly susceptible to external forces. To thrive in this dynamic environment, finance professionals must keep pace with industry trends and changes. Continuous learning is vital for several reasons:

- Market Dynamics: Financial markets can change rapidly due to geopolitical events, economic indicators, or market sentiment. To make informed decisions, financial experts must be up-to-date with these changes.

-       Regulatory   Changes: Governments and regulatory bodies often update financial regulations. Staying   compliant   and understanding these regulations is crucial to avoid legal issues and to ensure ethical business practices.

- Technological Advancements: The fintech industry is growing rapidly, introducing innovative tools and platforms. Professionals must be knowledgeable about these technologies to remain competitive.

- Globalization: The interconnectedness of global economies means that finance professionals must understand international markets and their dynamics.

2. Methods of Continuous Learning:

Professionals in finance have various options to engage in continuous learning:

- Formal Education: Pursuing advanced degrees like an MBA or financial certifications such as CFA, CPA, or CFP provides structured learning and in-depth knowledge.

- Seminars and Workshops: Attending industry-related seminars, workshops, and conferences is an excellent way to gain insights into the latest developments and network with peers.

- Online Courses and Webinars: The rise of online learning platforms has made it easier for finance professionals to access courses on a wide range of topics, often at their own pace.

- Reading and Research: Subscribing to financial publications, academic journals, and books can provide valuable insights. Research is key to staying informed.

- Mentorship and Networking: Building a strong professional network and seeking mentorship from experienced individuals can provide practical knowledge and guidance.

3. Adaptation in Finance:

Adaptation in finance involves applying newly acquired knowledge to address the changing financial landscape. Here are some key aspects of adaptation:

- Portfolio Management: Continuous learning helps investment professionals adapt their portfolio strategies to changing market conditions, risk profiles, and investor preferences.

- Risk Management: Adapting to

new risk factors and modeling techniques is essential for mitigating potential financial risks.

- Financial Technology: Embracing fintech innovations such as blockchain, AI, and robo-advisors is crucial for financial institutions to remain competitive and provide better services to clients.

- Compliance and Regulations: Adapting to new financial regulations and ensuring that compliance measures are in place are essential for avoiding legal issues and maintaining a positive reputation.

- Data Analysis and Interpretation: The ability to collect, analyze, and interpret financial data is a vital skill, especially as the amount of data available continues to grow.

4. The Benefits of Continuous Learning and Adaptation:

The advantages of prioritizing continuous learning and adaptation in finance are numerous:

- Competitive Advantage: Those

who stay current and adapt to changes are more likely to remain competitive and relevant in the industry.

- Risk Mitigation: Knowledge of financial markets and instruments can help professionals make informed decisions and reduce financial risks.

- Career Progression: Continuous learning often leads to career growth, better job opportunities, and increased earning potential.

- Client Trust: Clients are more likely to trust professionals who demonstrate a commitment to staying informed and providing the best advice.

- Innovation: Adapting to new technologies and trends can lead to the development of innovative financial products and services.

5. Challenges in Continuous Learning:

While the benefits are clear, there are challenges to continuous learning in finance:

- Time Constraints: Finance professionals often have demanding schedules, which can make it difficult to allocate time for learning.

- Information Overload: The abundance of information can be overwhelming, making it essential to discern what's most relevant.

- Costs: Pursuing formal education or attending conferences can be expensive.

- Resistance to Change: Some may

be resistant to adapting to new technologies or strategies, fearing the unfamiliar.

Continuous learning and adaptation are not just ideals but necessities in the world of finance. Those who embrace lifelong learning, stay informed about industry trends, and adapt to changes will be better positioned for success in this dynamic field. The financial landscape will continue to evolve, and finance professionals who make learning and adaptation a priority will not only survive but thrive in the ever-changing world of finance.

9.3 Preparing for the Post-Recession Future

Preparing for the Post-Recession Future

The world has experienced its fair share of economic recessions and downturns, and each time, societies have had to adapt and find ways to recover. The post-recession future is a period of uncertainty and transformation, but it also presents opportunities for growth and innovation. Here, we will explore key strategies and considerations for individuals, businesses, and governments to prepare for the post -recession future.

1. Diversify Your Skillset

As we emerge from a recession, the job market may be highly competitive. It's crucial to invest in your skillset to remain relevant. Consider acquiring new skills, taking online courses, or seeking additional certifications. Diversifying your skills can make you a more valuable asset to employers and increase your employability.

2. Reevaluate Financial Goals

A recession can have a significant impact on personal finances. Take this opportunity to reevaluate your financial goals, budget, and savings plan. Prioritize building an emergency fund, paying down debt, and investing wisely. It's also essential to adapt to new financial realities, which may include changing spending habits and setting achievable financial targets.

3. Entrepreneurship and Innovation

Economic downturns can be breeding grounds for entrepreneurship. New opportunities often arise from the ashes of a recession. If you have a business idea, consider taking the plunge. Governments and organizations may provide support and incentives for startups. Innovate and adapt to changing market conditions.

4. Strengthen Safety Nets

Recessions highlight the importance of strong safety nets. Governments should invest in social programs and unemployment benefits to protect vulnerable populations during economic hardships. These measures not only alleviate suffering but also stabilize the economy by maintaining consumer spending.

5. Sustainability and Resilience

Post-recession planning should prioritize sustainability and resilience. This means building a more robust and sustainable economy that can withstand future shocks. Focus on renewable energy, environmentally responsible practices, and supply chain resilience. Businesses and governments should incorporate these principles into their long-term strategies.

6. Embrace Remote Work and Technology

The COVID-19 pandemic accelerated the adoption of remote work and digital technologies. The post-recession future will likely continue this trend. Embrace technology, invest in digital infrastructure, and adapt to remote work arrangements. This can improve efficiency, reduce costs, and provide more flexibility in the workplace.

7. Strengthen International Partnerships

In an increasingly interconnected world, international cooperation is vital. Trade relationships and diplomacy play a significant role in economic recovery. Nations should work together to develop trade agreements, improve global supply chains, and address international challenges collectively.

8. Mental Health and Well-being

The psychological toll of a recession is often overlooked. Preparing for the post-recession future should include strategies to support mental health and well-being. Employers can offer counseling services and flexible work arrangements to alleviate stress. Individuals should prioritize self-care and seek help when needed.

9. Reskilling and Upskilling

Businesses should invest in reskilling and upskilling their workforce to remain competitive. Governments can facilitate this by providing training programs and incentives for companies to train employees. Preparing the workforce for the jobs of the future is crucial in a post-recession economy.

10. Crisis Preparedness

Recessions are a reminder that unforeseen crises can happen. Develop crisis preparedness plans for businesses and governments. This includes building a financial buffer, diversifying supply chains, and creating contingency plans for various scenarios.

Preparing for the post-recession future requires a multi-faceted approach. It involves personal and professional development, economic policy adjustments, and a commitment to sustainability and innovation. By taking these steps, individuals, businesses, and governments can not only recover from a recession but also thrive in the uncertain yet promising future. Remember that each recession is unique, but the lessons learned from past experiences can guide us in navigating the challenges and opportunities that lie ahead.

Conclusion:

Budgeting during a recession demands diligence, adaptability, and resilience. By understanding the economic landscape, creating a recession-proof budget, and making informed financial decisions, you can navigate these challenging times successfully. Remember, financial stability is not a sprint but a marathon. With the right strategies, you can emerge stronger and more financially secure in the post-recession world.